What are people saying?

"Coach Laughter is a trusted coach and friend, and The Athletes Challenge is a simple and useful tool for the everyday, packed full of wisdom, that will impact every coach, athlete, and team on and off the field."

Brad Cooper
Lead Pastor
NewSpring Church

"Coach Laughter has been an instrumental part of my life and a big part of my development as not only a coach but as a husband and father. The lessons and principles that he taught me playing for him I still carry to this day. The biggest compliment you can give any coach/leader is that they can relate and motivate people from all different backgrounds. Coach Laughter is a master at getting people to pull together towards one common goal and striving to be the best version of themselves."

Robert Livingston
Secondary/Safeties Coach
Cincinnati Bengals

"I have been fortunate enough to have known BJ for over 15 years. Over the years we have had a ton of great conversations about helping young people grow in their faith. Proverbs 22:6 tells us to train a child in the way he should go and when he is old, he will not depart from it. I believe this is one of the most powerful verses in scripture. Our young people are our future and as Christians, we must train them in a manner that is conducive and pleasing to Christ. With that being said, I believe that BJ Laughter has taken this scripture literally throughout his coaching career. Due to BJ's heart for developing young people for Christ, I do not doubt that this book will be a guiding light for young people for years to come."

Mike Clowney
Head Football Coach
Carson-Newman University

The Athlete's Challenge!

Where Athletic Ability, Character, and
Faith Combine!

Foreword by Sam Gash, Superbowl
Champion Fullback, Baltimore Ravens

BJ Laughter

Laughter/New Harbor Press
1601 Mt. Rushmore Rd, Ste 3288
Rapid City, SD 57701
www.NewHarborPress.com

Ordering Information:
Quantity sales. Special discounts are available on quantity pur-
chases by corporations, associations, and others. For details,
contact the "Special Sales Department" at the address above.

The Athlete's Challenge! / BJ Laughter -- 1st ed.
ISBN 978-1-63357-394-9

To Amy and Emma for always
believing in me. I love you guys!

Contents

Preface

There is no better platform in the world to reach people for Jesus Christ than athletics! This challenge is designed to create a generation of young people who want to glorify God in all realms of their life.

After a 30-year career in education, 23 of those years as a coach, I have a heart for athletes becoming all they can be in their skill, character, and faith life. I love to see student-athletes giving all the glory to God in everything they do in their lives, whether it be school, community, family life, or sports. This challenge is a two-week journey for any athlete to help them blend their faith and athletic ability into something special. Each day will have an athletic and spiritual challenge to help each student-athlete reach their full potential as a person. This challenge is designed with the busy athlete in mind and only asks for a 20-to-30-minute commitment each day for 14 days. It can be done alone, with a partner, with a group, or as a team. Each section has tough questions to answer as you look to enhance not only your athletic ability, but your role on your team, at your school, with your families, in your communities, and in the kingdom of God. God bless you!

Foreword

BJ Laughter is one of the greatest people I have ever had the pleasure of knowing. I was thrilled when my friend of over 40 years asked me to write a forward for his book.

I was born and raised in Hendersonville, NC, and graduated with BJ from Hendersonville High School in 1987. We both went on to the next level to play football, the game we loved. I was blessed to play for Coach Joe Paterno at Penn State from 1987 to- the Fall of 1991. After graduation in the Fall of 1991, I was drafted in the 8th round in the spring 1992 NFL draft, and I was blessed to play Fullback for 12 years in the NFL. (1992-1997 the New England Patriots, 1998-1999, 2003 the Buffalo Bills, making the Pro Bowl after the 1998 & 1999 seasons, 2000-2002 the Baltimore Ravens, winning Super Bowl XXXV January 28th, 2001).

Growing up in a small town, I stood out a little because I was big; I weighed 95 pounds in kindergarten and 120 pounds by the time I was in the second grade. I had very low self-esteem. BJ's Dad (Coach Jim Laughter- God Rest!) was my PE teacher in those early impressionable years. He instilled confidence, determination, and poise under pressure every day in me. Regardless of color, size, or family background, he treated us all with dignity and pushed us forward in whatever we were doing at the time. His older brother, Franklin, was one of my first ever basketball coaches. Franklin was a calming force as a coach that expected us to give our best effort when we were on the court and always seemed to be positive in his message being conveyed. His brother Chris was the fire that balanced us out! It was a great introduction to sports at the age of 8. They truly cared about winning, but if we lost (which was not very often), they were the same people after the game, just with things for us to work on. It was an awesome first sports experience. It showed me a lot going forward. Practices were tough, lots of running, which seemed even more as a hefty kid, but all the Laughters pushed me comfortably outside my comfort zone, with God's guidance. They are three of my early Saints! BJ has been and is that same light to the thousands of kids he has touched, just like his father.

My first recollection of BJ was at Boyd Park (Hendersonville Putt-Putt course across from the high school) with Mr. Laughter in charge. It was early one summer morning in the late '70s, we were eight years old, and our Mom (Betty Gash) had to be working. Sometimes we would go places and then be back by the time she got home from work, or at least be close by. She liked us within yelling distance! I went to the Putt-Putt spot with my cousin, Clifton Etheridge (Pooch), my younger brother (Eric Gash), who is 13 months younger, and our buddy Scott King (All-State Hooper). We all knew BJ from Bruce Drysdale school, and it just flowed like water with all of us clicking and getting along from that point on in time. BJ was on the smaller side, but you better not tell him that. He was a tough, scrappy guy that competed hard! We played basketball, raced each other, and played putt-putt some days. BJ got along with everyone the same. He has always had a great sense of humor, with the uncanny ability to be a joker and make everyone laugh, not just some. He has always seen people for their character and never for their color. I am so proud that he won so much as a coach, but even more proud of the lives he has affected in a positive light. Every student of his said lots of great things about him every time I would visit while I was in the NFL and after. He leads by example daily.

My brother Eric is a Minister (Speak Life Ministries located in Hendersonville, NC) who walks and talks God-talk and has done it from an early age. I love my Bro! Eric loves preaching and helping others. He is a principal at Bruce Drysdale, yes, our old school, and he took over once BJ left there as principal. Eric tells me how revered BJ was, and it makes all of us proud. He is my friend, and his life has been very much like my brothers in service of the Lord. BJ's writing a book, and Eric is running for Congress. Both are always aspiring to great things and are diligent, hard-working, and honor God in everything they do.

BJ has figured a great formula to make everyone be as God expected them to be. Read this book, follow what you read, and I promise your life will be enlightened and your outlook can be limitless to be whatever you feel the Lord is leading you to be.

Looking back on how things went for me growing up, God put BJ and his family in my life to help me gain the confidence needed to be great at whatever it was that I was doing or going to do. I believe BJ can be that light and beacon for God in today's world! People need a nice easy read that means something.

Sam Gash
All-Pro and 2001 Super Bowl Champion Fullback

Servant Leader

A servant leader is a leader compelled by the unshakable desire to serve! Servant leaders don't do things to draw attention to themselves; they do things from the goodness of their heart, not caring who gets the credit for it. It is their true desire to genuinely serve others without the expectation of reciprocation. This is the purest form of leadership and was demonstrated in the Bible many times by Jesus Christ. It reminds me of a player I had named Robert Livingston. He was the quarterback and free safety on one of the best teams I ever coached. He would always go the

extra mile in our locker rooms and athletic fields,
serving his teammates. Whether it was cleaning
up trash on the practice field or taking his teammates home after practice, he did it for the right
reasons and expected nothing in return. He was
one of the most unselfish people I have ever been
around. He did things for people that he knew
could not ever pay him back. That is one of the
number one characteristics of a true servant
leader! The whole team looked up to him, not
only for his athletic ability but for what he did as
a leader. Those characteristics Robert possesses
helped catapult him quickly through the coaching ranks, as he is now an assistant coach for
the Cincinnati Bengals in the National Football
League. I will always believe that his work ethic, desire, and genuine love of other people, as
demonstrated by how he served them when I was
around him, played a role in becoming the man
he is today. **Matthew 6:4** says, "So that your giving
may be done in secret, and God, who sees everything, will reward you!" **Philippians 2:3** says, "Do
nothing out of selfish ambition or vain conceit,
rather in humility, value others above yourself."
Luke 9:48 says, "The one who is least among you
is greatest." **Matthew 22:37–38** says, "Love the

Lord your God with all your heart, soul, mind, and love your neighbor as yourself!"

The three best practices of a servant leader:

1. **Servant leaders add value to others** – They let people know that they matter! One of the most profound moments in my life was my senior year at Mars Hill University. My last exam as a college student was in a classroom down in our football facility area. It was one of my hardest exams, and the last question on the exam was, "What is the name of the custodian who takes care of this building?" I was dumbfounded because I had no clue of what this gentleman's name was. It hit home with me because I had walked by that man every day for four years; I contributed to the mess that he had to clean up, throwing tape and Gatorade cups on the ground, and never being grateful to him or acknowledging that he even existed! Later in my career when I became an elementary school principal, one of the first things I implemented with the students at my school was the

importance of knowing the names of all those that served you and adding value to their lives by letting them know that they matter!

2. **Servant leaders express gratitude in all things** - An attitude of gratitude is present in any servant leader that I have ever been around. They seek out and acknowledge people that have done something to benefit them. Whether it be parents, friends, teachers, coaches, or teammates, they always express gratitude to others when they know they have been served. An attitude of gratitude will make you one of the most positive people in any room. People are drawn to positive people! Thank people when they do something nice for you, let them know that what they did for you was a big deal and that it did not go unnoticed!

3. **Servant leaders serve unconditionally-** Servant leaders seek out ways in which they can serve those they are around. It doesn't matter if they're the same color, race, or creed. It doesn't matter if they have things in common with them or if they're the same age or from the same

country. Servant leaders serve everyone unconditionally! Unexpected, undeserved, unrewarded acts of kindness will never come back void. Servant leaders serve unconditionally without the expectation of reciprocation.

These three practices are the cornerstones of being a servant leader. Today's challenge is for you to be intentional about being a servant leader at your school, in your community, in your family, and on your sports teams.

Reflection

In what areas do you need to improve as you strive to become a servant leader?

Is there someone serving you that you have not acknowledged? Maybe a custodian, cafeteria worker, store clerk, parent, teacher, coach, friend, etc.? Make a list and be intentional in seeking them out to acknowledge them.

Write down some strategies that you can implement in your athletic and faith journey that can help you be intentional about serving others without expectation of anything in return. Help those that have no way of ever paying you back!

Servant Leader Notes:

Focus and Character

Focus is the center of interest or activity, paying particular attention to something. Character is who you are when no one is looking. It has been said that your thoughts lead to your words, your words lead to your actions, your actions can determine your habits, and your habits determine your character. **Proverbs 10:9** says, "Whoever walks in integrity and character walks securely but whoever takes crooked paths will be found out!" In

2012 I was humbled and privileged to coach in the North Carolina versus South Carolina High School Shrine Bowl football game. It pitted the best players in the state of North Carolina versus the best players in the state of South Carolina. Many of the young men on the field that day went on to play college football on full scholarships, and some of those players even ended up in the NFL. One player, in particular, Noah Suber, was one of the quarterbacks that we selected for the North Carolina team. He was a quarterback at one of our local high schools, T.C. Roberson High, in Asheville, North Carolina. One day after a Shrine Bowl practice, a coach named Mike Clowney, an assistant coach at Carson- Newman University, approached me and asked if I could speak to their head coach, Ken Sparks, after practice regarding Noah. I, of course, said yes, I would love to talk to Coach Sparks about Noah! For the rest of the practice, I had in my mind the type of questions that Coach Sparks would ask. I was ready to answer all of the skill-related questions I thought were coming my way. Noah was so talented and gifted in his athletic abilities, so I thought this would be so easy and fun. After practice, I met with Coach Sparks and was thrown off by the type of questions that he asked. Coach Sparks did not ask one question about Noah's football ability. He asked me character-related questions, such as: How did he treat those serving him meals? How did he act in the locker room? How did he act in the hotel during his free time? How did he take coaching from the other coaches at practice? Was there any adversity during practice? How did Noah handle that adversity? I was able to answer those questions with great responses because Noah had more character than just about any player I had ever been around! The next day, Noah approached me and said that Carson-Newman had extended him a scholarship offer! I was reminded of a valuable lesson that day, that football is more than just wins and losses, that it is more than just athletic ability. Coach Sparks only asked questions about his character. Coach Sparks knew that he would have to spend the next four years with this young man and did not want to spend it with someone of low character that could cause him and his program problems. You see, what I learned from this was that your character determines your focus. As I reflect on my coaching career, the athletes who had great character had a different focus than those with low character. The high character athletes always focused on grades, relationships, bettering themselves as an athlete, and serving others! Low character athletes focused mostly on themselves! They focused on things like where is the next party, their statistics, and who they could get over on. Coach Sparks knew this and only recruited the highest of character student-athletes. I'm sure this is one of the main reasons that Coach Sparks is in the top five all-time in NCAA wins, with five national championships under his belt!

Help your character determine what you focus on!

1. **Eliminate distractions** – Eliminate things from your life that can distract you from your goals in school, athletics, family life, and your faith journey! You wouldn't want your surgeon watching TV as he performed your procedure, would you?

2. **You can't do too much** - You don't want to be decent at a bunch of things and good at none! Narrow your focus down to what's important to you at your particular time in life. If you are a student-athlete, that

means focusing on God, family, school, and athletics. Anything else can cause system overload and reduce the quality of work and focus on the most important things in your life.

3. **Focus on Jesus Christ** - Focus on Jesus in all you do! In **Matthew 14:29–30**, Peter was walking on the water to Jesus when he started to focus on the wind and the waves and took his eyes off Jesus. Peter immediately began to sink in the water! Peter let the distraction around him take his focus off of what was important, and he began to sink! Developing a strong relationship with Jesus Christ will build the character you need to focus on the things in your life to make you successful!

Proverbs 4:25 says, "Let your eyes look straight ahead; fix your gaze directly before you." **Colossians 3:2** says, "Set your mind on things above, not on earthly things."

Reflection

Are there any flaws in your character that you need to give attention to? List them.

It has been said that you are an average of the five people that you hang around most! Write down your five. Is this a good thing or a bad thing for you?

What currently has your focus? What steps can you take to change your focus if it is not where it needs to be in all areas of your life?

Focus and Character Notes:

Don't Flinch

To flinch is to make a quick, nervous movement as an instinct to fear, pain, or surprise. I think it was Mike Tyson that once said, "Everyone has a plan until they get punched in the face!" That is so true in sports and life! We all have an idea of how things are supposed to go, and then all of a sudden, something punches you in the face, whether it be the death of a loved one, disease, failing a class, loss of a job, divorce, etc. The same holds true in the sports world. You think you have a good game plan, you've prepared hard at practice, and then something happens all of a sudden, and it smacks you in the face. In my first year ever as a head football coach, we were on the road at Murphy High School. Murphy is a perennial state title contender, and we were losing 27 to 0 at halftime. I was a first-year head coach, and their coach is the winningest coach of all time in North Carolina high school football history! We were smacked in the face, and our team, as well as our coaching staff, had a sense of doom! Even though I was a first-year head coach, our players had a sense of mental toughness that year and did not panic in the face of that adversity. To make a long story short, we scored with about five seconds left in the game to make it Murphy 27, Hendersonville 26. I huddled with our team on the sidelines, and they decided that they wanted to go for two for the win since we were on the road and did not want to go into overtime. We ran a toss sweep to Vincent Neclos, one of the best running backs I've ever coached, and he ran right at the orange pylon on the corner of the front right of the end zone. He got in for the two-point conversion, and we ended up completing one of the biggest comebacks in our school's history, on the road at one of the toughest opponents in North Carolina. Our team did not flinch!

The Bible speaks about not flinching. **Philippians 1:28** from The Message says, "not flinching or dodging in the slightest before the opposition. Your courage and unity will show them what they are up against, defeat for them and victory for you both because of God!" The Bible is an instruction book for all of us. Now I'm sure that the Bible was not talking about football in this verse but talking about life. That's why I love sports so much because it teaches you how to deal with adversity, so when life's real problems hit you, you won't flinch or dodge in the slightest because you know God has your back. When you have a relationship with Jesus Christ, He sends the Holy Spirit into your heart, and that is the rock to build your life around! God doesn't promise that everything will be all right here on Earth, but He does promise that we will be all right for eternity! As **Romans 8:31** states, "If God is for us, who can be against us?"

Don't Flinch!

Any adversity in life or sports is the opposition. Putting God first in your life will give you the mindset to be a warrior in the face of adversity, whether it be in an athletic contest or dealing with how harsh life can be. Don't flinch because you have the DNA of the creator of the universe pumping through your blood!!

Reflection

Death, sickness, problems on your team/sport, divorce, relationship problems, home problems, getting bullied, addiction, disappointment, financial situations, etc., are all "stuff" that can cause us to flinch and get discouraged and lose hope and faith. What are some things that make you flinch that you need to lay at the feet of Jesus to overcome? No matter how bad it is, Jesus will get you to the other side of it!

Pay attention! You might be OK, but are there friends, family members, teammates that are going through things that can make them flinch that you can come alongside and help them through it?

Start a relationship with Jesus if you have not already, and start your day with Him in reading and prayer! Be intentional with asking him for

help with things that cause you to have adversity!
If you don't ask, the answer is always no!

Don't Flinch Notes:

Warriors

A warrior is a person engaged or experienced in warfare. A warrior is a person engaged in some struggle or conflict. On November 9, 2012, at Hendersonville High's Dietz Field, my football team was trailing 34 to 7 at halftime in a second-round playoff game to Lake Norman Charter School. When we came out for the opening kick of the second half, we noticed more than half of the fans on our side had left. It was a packed house that night, so it was obvious to see everyone had lost faith in our team. I don't blame them; I probably would've left too. We couldn't do anything right, and we were playing sluggishly. However, this team was different with a group of seniors led by quarterback Grant Rivers, who had a true warrior mindset. At halftime, instead of screaming and yelling and pointing blame at each other, we got everyone calmed down, put in a few minor adjustments that we could execute, and we went out for the second half. Our strategy was simple: stop them, get a score, then do that over and over again. It was amazing, we scored 27 points in the third quarter, 14 more points in the fourth quarter, and we held Lake Norman to just six points the entire second half. It was the biggest comeback in school history! We won 48 to 40 and advanced to the state quarterfinals. The amazing thing in that game wasn't just that we came back, but watching the stands fill back up by the end of the third quarter. Our fans were listening on the radio, and when they heard us coming back, they filed back into the stadium. It was beautiful! As the game was ending, our stands were packed again! I don't tell the story to brag on my coaching prowess or brag on that team that year; I tell the story because this group of student-athletes were warriors! They weren't just warriors on the football field; they were warriors in the classroom and their community, and our quarterback, Grant, was a true warrior for Jesus Christ! In **Joshua 1:9,** it says, "Have I not commanded you? Be strong and courageous. Don't be afraid or discouraged, for the Lord your God is with you wherever you go." Our players controlled their effort, attitude, and their preparation. Those are warrior qualities. Even if we had lost that game, that group of young men had those qualities, they didn't get discouraged, and they stayed courageous! As a coach, you want your players to have that warrior mindset. Mental toughness is only revealed when you face pressure, adversity, or disappointment. Some unhealthy ways to respond to adversity in sports are to cry, complain, go through the motions, get on social media with drama, or simply quit. When adversity strikes in life, some people choose things like divorce, withdrawal, substance abuse, physical abuse, neglect, blame others or God, etc. Through my experience in coaching, education, and life, these negative responses to adversity usually show up when Jesus Christ is not at the center of a person's life.

Be a warrior in sports and life!

1. **Warriors refuse to make excuses-** True warriors refuse to make excuses. They look for practical solutions to their problems. They realize that the blame game never works, and making excuses never cures anything.

2. **Warriors rise in tough situations-** True warriors are the ones who step it up in tough situations. They want the ball, they want to be on the foul line, they want to be set up, they want to be at-bat, they want to be the anchor leg, and they want to come through for their team when it counts. Athletes that have God in their lives realize that they are performing for the glory of the creator of the universe! An athlete with that Christian mindset understands the gift that God has given them, and they want to come through not only for their team but for God!

3. **Warriors recover from setbacks-** Athletes that have Christ in their lives understand that a setback is a set up for an amazing comeback! **John 16:33** says, "I have told you

all this so that you may have peace in me. Here on Earth, you will have trials and sorrows, but take heart because I have overcome the world." In **James 1:2-4**, it says, "Consider it pure joy, my brothers and sisters, whenever you face trials of many kinds because you know that the testing of your faith produces perseverance. Let perseverance finish its work so that you may be mature and complete, not lacking anything." Warriors are the athletes who can shake it off when they get burned for a touchdown, strikeout, get aced, drop a baton, fumble, etc.

4. **Warriors put God first in all they do!**

Reflection

Are there any situations in your life where you need to develop this warrior mindset?

How do you respond when things don't go your way? Pouting? Anger? Blaming? Quitting?

What do you turn to in times of adversity? If you don't already, I encourage you to turn to Jesus

Christ in times of adversity. The Bible gives us instructions on how to deal with adversity! **James 1:2. Joshua 1:9. Deuteronomy 31:6,8.**

Surround yourself with solid people!

Warriors! Notes:

Uncommon Effort

An effort is a vigorous or determined attempt, strenuous physical or mental exertion. As a head football coach, I had many different players who gave effort and all they had, and I admire that so much in a young person. Many famous coaches have said that "It doesn't take any talent to hustle," and I always believed that if I could take my average players and make them better than your average players, we would win more games than we lose. I loved it when I found a player that would give everything they had regardless of the situation. They would give all they had if they were in a bad mood, sick, hurt, or not feeling 100%. One player I coached comes to mind when I think of uncommon effort. AJ McMinn was a fullback for me at Hendersonville High School. He ended up playing on a full scholarship at North Carolina A&T State University, starting almost every game as a fullback, blocking for Tarik Cohen, who was drafted in the third round by the Chicago Bears and became an All-Pro. What made AJ special was the effort that he gave at all times. He never loafed, he played hurt, he played sick, he played if he had a bad day, he always had a positive attitude, took coaching well, and the most important thing was AJ put God first in his life. AJ lived out **Colossians 3:23-24**, which says, "Whatever you do, work at it with all your heart, as working for the Lord, not humans, since you know you will receive an inheritance from the Lord as a reward. It is the Lord Christ you are serving." I love what Rick Barnes, the head basketball coach at Tennessee, used during one of his basketball seasons. His FCA representative, Chris Walker, talked about how they were going to play for an "audience of one." They talked about how, when they step into the arena, they envisioned it being empty, with God being the only person in attendance. They wanted to play to glorify Him and give all that they had. AJ reminded me of that with the way he played ball. I was the head coach at Hendersonville High School for 17 years and I cannot remember another player that did not miss a practice or a game the entire four years. AJ did just that! That is the definition of uncommon effort to me. Uncommon effort is about energy! I love what Brad Cooper from NewSpring Church said:

"Low energy people kill momentum.

Low-energy people kill teams.

Low energy is about effort.

Effort is about choice, not talent."

There is no energy in logic, only in passion.

Be passionate in all that you do! Have high energy!

Worrying is believing God won't get it right!

Reflection

Every day ask yourself: Did you made anyone better today? Did you make your team better today?

Ken Smith said, "One person with goals, character, compassion, and discipline can make a difference on a team, in a church, at school, or in the world." I challenge you to make these characteristics describe yourself!

Give uncommon effort every rep, every assignment, every interaction with people, in your job, with your family, with friends, with Jesus. To resist what you know is wrong takes effort. Do what's right even if it's not popular!

Extra reading: **Galatians 6:9, Proverbs 13:4, Philippians 4:13, 1 Timothy 4:10**

Uncommon Effort Notes:

Execution

Execution is the carrying out or putting into effect a plan, order, or course of action. Back in the 1990s, I was coaching in a very critical football game on the road. The other team had been completing some underneath passes the whole game. We were in a 3-deep zone, which means three defenders have the deep thirds of the football field, and four defenders had the short zones underneath. We had some issues all season long with one of the deep defenders wanting to come out of his zone and try to defend the underneath stuff. If you have a deep responsibility and come up into the short zones, you put the team at risk of giving up a touchdown pass. It's easy for a young athlete to become frustrated watching pass after pass be completed in front of him. It makes him want to try to compensate for his teammate's job. The problem in sports is if you don't execute your job, and you try to compensate for someone else, then you end up hurting everyone! Long story short, we were ahead 14 to 13 with time quickly dissipating. The other team dropped back to pass, pump-faked into the flats, and threw a deep touchdown pass over one of our deep defenders who had bit up into the short zone to try to make a play. We lost that game 20 to 14! This was a classic example of what happens when someone on your team doesn't execute the job that has been assigned to them. Everyone suffers! I could've easily pointed fingers at the athlete, but that wasn't the reason we lost the game; that was just the last mistake made. If we don't execute our jobs in any phase of life, the result can lead to destruction. If we don't execute in our jobs, we can be fired. If we don't execute in our marriages, it can lead to divorce. If we don't execute in school, we can fail. If we don't execute taking care of our bodies, it can lead to health problems. If we don't execute accepting

Jesus as our Lord and Savior, it can cause us to be separated from God forever! The first person you need to evaluate before you worry about anyone else is yourself. **Matthew 7:3-4** says: "Why do you look at the speck of sawdust in your brother's eye and not pay attention to the plank in your eye? Can you say to your brother, let me take that speck out of your eye when all the time there is a plank in your eye?" Doing your job doesn't guarantee that you will be successful all the time, but it is still better than a mess!

To execute on any team or organization:

1. Always evaluate yourself first.
2. Approach people out of love, knowing all have fallen short. **Romans 3:23** says, "For **ALL** have sinned and fallen short of the glory of God."
3. Always do your job to the best of your ability. You cannot control anything else.

Reflection

What are some areas in your life that you could execute better?

What are some things you can do to be intentional about improving in these areas?

Do you have a relationship with Jesus Christ? Read **Romans 5:8, John 1:10-13, John 3:16, Revelation 3:20, Jeremiah 29:11, Hebrews 11:6.**

Execution Notes:

Work Ethic

Work ethic is the principle that hard work is intrinsically virtuous or worthy of reward. I always took pride as a head football coach in the fact that I was going to make my average players better than everyone else's average players. I always believed that was the key to winning. If you can take your players and make them better than they were when they first met you, you're going to be successful. We always tried to instill that in our players, that if they could outwork everyone else, it would give them a chance to win at a high level. One of the best examples of a strong work ethic paying off in sports was a player I coached named Tim Collman. He was only 5'9" and 160 pounds and not the most gifted athlete on the team, but he got the most out of what he did have. He never missed any training sessions, never missed school, never missed practice, and was highly coachable. He had a motor that never quit and was relentless in his pursuit to contribute to our team. In Tim's senior season, it paid off, and he ended up starting for me on the defensive line. He was an overachiever on a football team that won 14 games in 2003. He was named the defensive MVP for our team in the Western Championship game. His hard work paid off for him as well as our team. On that same team, we had a player named Charles "Momo" Featherstone. He was born with a club foot and had one leg smaller than the other. He stayed in pain on the football field, but his work ethic and his desire were unmatched. He played on both sides of the ball as a linebacker and a running back. He overcame so much because of his work ethic. He loved being out there and loved competing so much that he would do whatever it took to be on that field!

The Bible talks about work ethic in 2 Thessalonians 3:10, "For even when we were with you, we would give you this command: if anyone is not willing to work, let him not eat." This verse is so relevant to today's athletes. Many times, when we turn on the TV, we see athletes motioning like they are eating when they do something spectacular on the field or in the arena. This eating motion is kind of prophetic in athletics. For you to be able to perform on a level to where you're excelling in sports, it is going to take a tremendous work ethic. I always think about this verse in Thessalonians when I see an athlete make the "eating motion." Developing a work ethic in your daily life is also critical. **Proverbs 10:4** speaks to this. "A slack hand causes poverty, but the hand of the diligent makes rich." Work ethic in sports, your daily life, or your spiritual life has to be intentional. You have to get up every day, look at yourself in the mirror and decide whether or not you're going to work hard.

What can happen if you don't have work ethic in sports?

- You can be beaten by less talented teams or individuals.
- You can let your team and your teammates down.
- You will not live up to your potential.
- You will not grow and improve, which is devastating at the end of the season.
- Plans for the next level will never come to fruition.

What can happen if you don't have work ethic in your daily life?

- You will not live up to your earning potential.
- You can let your family down.
- You will set a bad example for those that look up to you.
- Education level can be affected.
- You can lose jobs or be labeled as lazy.
- Your future, as far as retirement and things like that, can be negatively affected.

And if you don't have a work ethic in your spiritual journey?

- You won't increase your knowledge of who Jesus is.
- Your relationship with Jesus can stall.
- You will increase the risk that you will revert to previous behaviors that could be destructive.

Coach Mark Richt once said that "It doesn't take talent to hustle!" The following is a list of things that take zero talent:

- Being on time
- Effort
- Body language
- Energy
- Attitude
- Passion
- Being coachable/teachable
- Doing extra
- Being prepared

Reflection

On a scale of 1 to 10, with 10 being the best and 1 being the worst, where would you rank your work ethic in the following three areas: sports, daily life, spiritual life?

Think about some strategies that you could intentionally use to get your ranking in those three areas as close to 10 as possible and write them down.

God wants us to maximize our abilities in everything we do! **1 Corinthians 10:31**: "So, whether you eat or drink, or whatever you do, do all to the glory of God."

Work Ethic Notes:

Choose Everyday

Joshua 24:15: "But if serving the Lord seems undesirable to you, then choose for yourselves this day whom you will serve, whether the gods your ancestors served beyond the Euphrates or the gods of the Amorites, in whose land you are living. But as for me and my household, we will serve the Lord." Joshua was saying to get in or get out. You can't stand somewhere in the middle! I heard Dr. Faris Jordan say one time at a clinic that he would "give $10,000 to anyone that could tell him something that they did, that they didn't want to do." People in the audience were giving responses such as, "I didn't want to bury my mom," and Dr. Jordan would say, "Yes, you did, or you could've left her in the house to rot!" I remember another person saying, "I didn't want to mow my grass," and Dr. Jordan said, "Yes, you did, or you could've just let everything grow up around your house and never cut it!" Dr. Jordan went on to explain that wanting to do something doesn't mean that you have to like it. He explained that once you understand that concept, that was the cornerstone of mental health. He had the stance that we want to do everything that we do, or we wouldn't do it. Everything that we do is a choice. We will make thousands of choices every day for the rest of our lives. When we realize that we want to make those choices, it will make us have an attitude of gratitude. Instead of saying, "I didn't want to bury my mom, I didn't want to go to the dentist, I didn't want to mow my grass, I didn't want to go to school," we can take the posture of "Thank God that I have the means to bury my mom, thank God that I can go to the dentist, thank God that I'm able to mow my grass, thank God that I get to go to school." This is the healthy way to approach choices that you have to make in your life. It makes you thankful for everything that you have.

In sports:

- Choose to go hard or not.
- Choose to be a good teammate or not.
- Choose to accept your role on your team or not.
- Choose to be coachable or not.

In your daily life:

- Choose to participate in school or not.
- Choose to study and do your work or not.
- Choose to behave or not.
- Choose to listen to your parents or not.
- Choose to hang around good people or not.
- Choose to listen to wise people or not.

In your faith journey:

Very simply, choose to follow Jesus or not, at all times, not blending in.

Following Christ, being great, being a good person, is a daily choice!

Reflection

Are there better choices that you need to be making in your sports life?

Are there better choices that you need to be making in your daily life?

Have you chosen to follow Jesus at all times without blending in? If not, you can choose that right now, today!

Choose Everyday Notes:

Iron Sharpens Iron

I've heard it said by many different people that you are an average of the five people you spend the most time with. For some people, that can be an amazing thing, while it can be a scary thought for others. They say, "Iron sharpens iron," but if you're not around the kind of people that can sharpen you and you can sharpen them, then it's probably not a great relationship. I've also heard people say things like, "Show me your friends and

I'll show you your future," "The fleas come with the dog," "If you hang out with poop, you'll eventually smell like poop!" The Bible speaks about friends and surrounding yourself with good people. **Proverbs 17:17** says, "A friend loves at all times." **Proverbs 18:25** says, "One who has unreliable friends soon comes to ruin." **John 15:13** says, "Greater love has no one than this: to lay down one's life for one's friend." Many times during my coaching career, I would have an athlete on my team that was just an awesome friend and teammate, a great citizen at school and in the community, but as soon as the season was over and they got away from that great group of friends they were hanging around, they fell back into bad habits. Some of those habits included: failing classes, office referrals, trouble with substances and alcohol, and trouble with the authorities. As a high school coach, it was hard to keep those friend groups together after the season. We would try to encourage our student-athletes to have a good friend group, but in the end, everyone has to choose for themselves. I challenge any athlete reading this to evaluate your friend groups and decide what action you should take. You cannot be an excellent student-athlete and participate in unhealthy things. In the end, you get exposed, and the consequences can be devastating. Develop your friend group based on biblical principles. The Bible is a good instruction manual for how to live your life. If you want to be the best student-athlete that you can be, keep God first in all that you do and seek out friends that keep God first in all that they do.

Better friends =

- Better teams
- Servant leaders
- Selflessness

Iron sharpens iron! Here are a few key characteristics of a true friend:

- Dependable during good or bad times
- Accountability- They call you out whether it is popular or not, in a loving way!
- Trustworthy- They keep your confidence; they won't go and tell others.
- Honest- once again, whether it is popular or not

- Generous- They will sacrifice for you without expectation of reciprocation.

Reflection

How would you describe the character of the five people you spend the most time with? Are there any relationships that you need to review?

How would you describe your character?

What are some things that you could do to make yourself a better teammate? If iron truly sharpens iron, are you the iron for someone else?

Iron Sharpens Iron Notes:

Tenacity

Tenacity is the quality or fact of being very determined. Of all my years of coaching, there was one player that stands out in my mind when I hear the word tenacity. Chuck Freeman played football for me in the early 2000s as a defensive end and full back. Chuck wasn't the greatest natural athlete, he had average speed, average quickness, but he was so determined to improve and had a work ethic like nobody else. Chuck set a tone for us that season that no coach or any other player could set. He went so hard at practice that the other players actually despised him sometimes because he would not let up, and it would make them look bad if they let up. It forced our team to go harder because if they didn't go hard, Chuck would make them look foolish. He never went half speed in any drill, no matter what day it was or how he felt. The frustration he caused led to great conversations among our team, which in turn made us practice harder as a unit, and we beat some teams that year that we had no business beating because one player decided to play hard at all times. Tenacity is contagious! When players on any team are tenacious, it makes other players become tenacious, which spreads and makes your team tenacious. Chuck Freeman ended up being an all-conference football player for us. He won his all-conference spot over some players in our conference that were much more talented than he was, and he did it from just sheer desire to be the best that he could be. He was the definition of being very determined. The Bible talks about being determined and tenacious. 2 Timothy 4:7 says, "I have fought the good fight, I have finished the race, I have kept the faith." The Bible teaches us that we should have tenacity in everything that we do! You can't just have tenacity when everything is going your way. You have to have tenacity during the good times and the bad times, no matter the situation. The Bible teaches us that!

Don't let your mood dictate your level of tenacity! Be determined to be your best even if you have a headache, failed a test, are in a bad mood, having troubles at home, etc.

People with a high level of tenacity:

- Have the courage to stand strong in hard times in athletics and life.
- Have amazing endurance.
- Never waiver on their faith in Jesus Christ.

Reflection

How would your teammates, coaches, and teachers describe you and your level of tenacity? What would you want them to say?

How would your family describe your level of tenacity? What would you want them to say?

If you could talk to Jesus Christ right now, face-to-face, how would he describe your level of tenacity? What would you want Him to say?

What are some things you can do to increase your level of tenacity?

Tenacity Notes:

Unity

Unity is the state of being united or joined as a whole. Uniformity is remaining the same in all cases at all times. As a head football coach, it was sometimes hard to get my teams to understand the difference between unity and uniformity. A lot of players thought that we all had to believe in the same things. One big hurdle was getting our teams to understand that you can have differences in views and opinions and still be united. You can be from a different background, culture, race, speak a different language, and still be united. One big thing in developing unity with any team or organization is getting them to understand and appreciate the different points of view from those they are working with. You don't have to agree on everything to be a good friend or teammate. This is one concept that we would try to get our players to understand to develop great chemistry. One of my most skilled athletic teams ever in my coaching career had one of the worst records for the season. They had more athletic skill than just about everybody we played, but we lost to many teams that we should've beaten because we were always in an argument with each other. We had a lot of racial tension that year on our team, and we could never get them to understand that to be united, you don't have to be uniform. We worked on that the entire season, and we finally got them to believe in this concept on the last week of the season. We were 2-8 and hosting a team that was 10-0. We finally came together that week! You could see it developing at practice all week. Our players had been getting along, having fun together, and doing things together outside of the school environment. We ended up beating that team 39 to 19 in a huge upset! That set the tone for the entire off-season and into the next season. The following season, we ended up 11-2 and made a good playoff run. This was due to the unity developed the year before on the team with the worst record that I ever coached! **Psalm 133:1** speaks to this concept. The Psalm reads, "How good and pleasant is it, when God's people live together in unity."

You can still be united even if:

- Someone listens to different music from you.
- Someone comes from a different culture than you.
- Someone has different hobbies than you.
- Someone has different political views than you.
- Someone learns a different way than you, whether it be book smart, hands-on, etc.
- Someone is a different race than you.
- Someone has a different socio-economic background than you.

Every day get up and evaluate yourself. In heaven, there will be every type of person on the face of the earth, and they will be united in the common cause of Jesus Christ. We might as well get started here on earth now! We are all in the image of God! **Genesis 1:27** says, "So God created man in his image, in the image of God he created him; male and female he created them."

Reflection

Take an honest inventory of yourself. Can you get along with those that might not be just like you? That doesn't mean that you have to believe in what they believe in or compromise your faith. Jesus tells us to love our neighbors in **Mark 12:31**. "You shall love your neighbor as yourself. There is no other greater commandment than this." This verse didn't say love your neighbor if they are like you! I challenge you to be the athlete on your team that unifies your team. You may be the only Jesus that your teammates ever see!

Write down the names of three people you normally wouldn't hang out with and commit to get to know them this week.

Unity Notes:

Skin in the game

Having a vested interest in something means that a person or group has a personal stake or involvement in something. A good slang term for this is having "skin in the game." Most of the time, if someone is given something for free, they will not take as good care of it as they would if they had some money and time invested in it. I mean, if it tears up, they have lost nothing. The same holds true in sports. If you have worked to get where you are, it means something to you if it's no longer available to you. It's tragic to see an athlete work hard in the off-season, put in the time and effort, and then get injured and not be able to complete the season. It is devastating to someone who has put the time and effort in to not be able to reap the benefits of that hard work. On the other hand, if you're an athlete that has done nothing extra to prepare for the season and just show up when the season starts, it's not as big a deal if you can't play anymore, or lose, or have the season end without meeting your goals. It doesn't mean as much to an athlete who doesn't have "skin in the game." One of the best examples of this is my daughter. Emma joined the track team in her freshman year at Hendersonville High School. She had been a long and triple jumper in middle school, and in her eighth-grade year, she was the number one triple jumper in her middle school conference when she developed a stress fracture and was unable to finish the season. She never got a chance to try to win the conference. In high school, her legs couldn't take the pounding of triple jumping anymore, so she started trying pole vault. She loved how difficult it was and fell in love with it. She worked hard at practice and extra on the weekends and after hours. By the end of her freshman year, she finished sixth place at the outdoor 1A State meet in Greensboro. That off-season, she worked on her technique many days and many weekends, and her sophomore year, she won the State Championship at the indoor 1A/2A state track championships in Winston-Salem. Her leg started bothering her again before outdoor track started. She pushed through the pain and completed that season as well with a successful third-place finish at the state outdoor track meet in Greensboro. The harder she worked, the more her leg hurt, and by the end of the indoor meet her junior year in Winston-Salem, she was vaulting a foot less than the beginning of the season and finished seventh at the state meet. After many doctor visits, we finally found a doctor that diagnosed what was wrong with her leg. She had developed something called "Compartment Syndrome" in her shin from her stress fracture. The decision was a simple decision but heartbreaking, nonetheless. She could have surgery that could leave a big scar on her leg and still not be guaranteed that the pain would be gone, or she could simply quit running track. Emma decided to give it up. It was heartbreaking for her because she never got to see the potential that she could've reached in that event. She had a lot of skin in the game, so it meant a lot to her;

that's why it hurt so much not to be able to compete anymore. Skin in the game is talked about in our faith lives as well. In **Matthew 7:22-23**, it says, "Many will say Lord, Lord, didn't we prophesy in your name and drive out demons in your name and perform many miracles in your name? Then I will tell them plainly, 'Depart from me, I never knew you.'" This is the scariest verse in all the Bible for me because it talks about how serious it is to have "skin in the game" with Jesus. If you can't publicly profess him as your Lord and Savior, and follow him, and put him first in all that you do to glorify him, then he will say one day, "Depart from me I never knew you." Jesus Christ doesn't want us to be lukewarm in anything we do in our lives. The Bible speaks of this in **Revelation 3:15-16**: "I know your works: you are neither cold nor hot, so because you were lukewarm and neither hot nor cold, I will spit you out of my mouth." Coaches do not want you to be lukewarm on their teams. Teachers do not want you to be lukewarm in their classrooms. Your family does not want you to be lukewarm at home. And Jesus Christ, the creator of the universe, doesn't want you to be lukewarm when it comes to him. Whatever you do, decide to do it to the best of your ability, or don't do it.

Reflection

As an athlete, are you preparing for your sport year-round? Diet? Exercise? Mentally?

In school, are you doing all of your work and studying to the best of your ability?

At home, are you positively contributing to your family? In the community and on social media?

Are you lukewarm with Jesus Christ? Or are you following him and making it known publicly?

Skin in the Game Notes:

Process— "The Grind"

A process is a series of actions or steps taken to achieve a particular end. Clemson Football Head Coach Dabo Swinney always talks about enjoying the process instead of focusing on the end goal. What Coach Swinney is talking about here is that you have to enjoy the off-season conditioning and weight training, the rigor of your classwork in school, the film study, the spring practices, and all the ups and downs that come with being a student-athlete. If you don't fall in love with the process that many call "the grind," you can end up miserable and hating what you do. The Bible talks about the process in **Ecclesiastes 8:6**. It says, "For there is a proper time and procedure for every matter." This verse probably wasn't talking about sports, but it sure relates to your life. There are proper times for everything in your life. You don't want to spend your life trying to reach end goals and not enjoy the ride. My daughter is 21 years old now, and as I look back on the process of raising her, it makes me realize how valuable some of the things that I used to have to do were. The process of changing her diapers, taking care of her when she was sick, packing her lunch day after day, attending endless dance recitals and band concerts, trying every sport imaginable, putting up with her first boyfriend, worrying when she got her drivers' license, and dropping her off at college - I could go on and on, but you get the idea! You have to realize that the process is what you need to fall in love with in all that you do because that means you're loving every day of your life, not looking grudgingly ahead at what lies before you. Every process must have priorities. The following is a list of priorities that my college football coach, Felton Stephens, used to teach us to live by:

1. God
2. Family
3. Academics
4. Athletics

As a student-athlete, you should have your identity in Christ! Yes, you are an athlete, but when athletics is over, if you have all of your identity in that sport or sports, then there's going to be a void there. If you have your identity in Jesus Christ from the beginning, everything else you do is just a Christ-follower doing an activity. So, when the dust settles and your athletic career is over, you still have an identity in Christ Jesus, and sports don't define you. As you can see from the list above, athletics is pretty far down the list. To become the best student-athlete you can be, you always need to put God first, your family second, your schoolwork third, and then focus on athletics. Your leisure time, friends, hobbies all have to come after those four things. If you live in such a way where your priorities get out of order, stress can set in, which can affect your performance not only in sports but in your family life, your academic life, and your faith life as well. Coach Stephens was really big on us living by our priorities because he knew it would make us much better student-athletes. When our priorities are in order, we're better followers of Christ, we're better family members, our grades go up, and we perform better in athletics and become very solid teammates.

Reflection

If you have never written down your priorities, I challenge you to do so now. Be very serious about it and give it a lot of thought. If you commit to living in all areas of your life based on these priorities, you will become a better student-athlete.

Are you following the process to be a student-athlete year-round? Some examples are weight training, conditioning, agility, speed work, studying schemes, technique, individual skills, academic effort, getting along with others, nutrition, practices, games, social life, positive social media, being a good family member, etc.

If you are not living out the process and enjoying every day, I would challenge you to take a deep look at what you're doing every day and make the necessary changes to become more effective in everything that you do.

Process — "The Grind" Notes:

Sense of Urgency

Urgency means that something is of utmost importance, requiring swift action. In the world of sports, some examples of needing to be urgent are play clocks, inbound time limits, five-second calls, 10-second calls, and the two-minute drill in football. The real world has its own examples of needing to be urgent. Deep cuts, broken bones, kidney stones, bill deadlines, projects due, big exams, college/scholarship applications, or simply being on time are just some of the examples of items that require swift action. When I heard the tragic news of Kobe Bryant and his daughter dying in a horrific helicopter crash, I couldn't help the questions and thoughts that I had going through my mind that whole week. The Bible says in **James 4:14** that life is vapor, "yet you do not know what your life will be like tomorrow. For you are just a vapor that appears for a little while and then vanishes away." Eternity is real, and we will be in eternity somewhere, whether it be heaven or hell. The Bible speaks about eternity in **John 5:24.** It says, "Truly, truly, I say to you, whoever hears my word and believes him who sent me has eternal life. He does not come into judgment but has passed from death to life." I couldn't help but think, was Kobe ready for eternity? Had he accepted Jesus Christ as his Savior? My mom and dad both passed away in the last five years, and I think I know where they are, but in the end, no one really knows except the individual. You see, we have to make that decision for ourselves. Whether we accept Christ or not is totally up to us. It doesn't matter if your grandmama taught Sunday school, or you went to Bible camp, or you were a good person most of the time. Your parents, your friends, your pastor, your youth leaders, don't save you. These people are great in your life, and they can lead you to Christ, but in the end, you have to ultimately decide whether or not you will accept Him as your Lord and Savior and follow him for the rest of your life. If you are a Christian, then it is your job to have a sense of urgency to make sure that you tell everybody you can the good news about Christ so they can have the opportunity to make the decision as well. The Bible plainly tells us as Christians what our main job is in **Matthew 28:16-20**. "Then the 11 disciples went to Galilee, to the mountain where Jesus had told them to go. When they saw him, they worshipped him; but some doubted. Then Jesus came to them and said, "all authority in heaven and on earth has been given to me. Therefore, go and make disciples of all nations, baptizing them in the name of the Father and of the Son and of the Holy Spirit, and teaching them to obey everything I have commanded you. And surely, I am with you always, to the very end of the age." If you are not a Christian, but you want to be, it is very easy. As a representative of the Fellowship of Christian Athletes, we use something called "The Four" to help you understand what God did for us through his son Jesus Christ, and what he offers us if we choose to accept Him. The Four:

1. **God loves you.** God made you and loves you! His love is boundless and unconditional. God is real, and he wants you to personally experience his love and discover his purpose in your life through a relationship with him. (**Genesis 1:27, John 3:16**)

2. **Sin separates you from God.** You cannot experience God's love when you ignore him. People search everywhere for meaning and fulfillment but not with God. They don't trust God and ignore his ways. The Bible calls this sin. Everyone has sinned. Sin damages your relationships with other people and with God. It keeps us from experiencing the fulfilling life that God intends for us. Result: you are eternally separated from God and the life he planned for you. (**Romans 3:23, Romans 6:23, Isaiah 59:2**)

3. **Jesus rescues you.** Sin does not stop God from loving you. Because of God's great love, he became a human being in Jesus Christ and gave his life for you. At the cross, Jesus took your place and paid the penalty of death that you deserve for your sins. Jesus died, but he rose to life again.

Jesus offers you peace with God and a personal relationship with him. Through faith in Jesus, you can experience God's love daily, discover your purpose and have eternal life after death. (**1 Peter 3:13, 1 Corinthians 15:38, Romans 5:8**)

4. **Will you trust Jesus?** You can place your trust in Jesus by faith through prayer. Prayer is talking with God. God knows your heart, and he's not concerned with your words as much as he is with the attitude of your heart.

Here's a suggested prayer: Dear God, thank you for loving me and wanting the best for my life. I live my life for myself and do things my way, and I am truly sorry. Jesus, I believe that you are God and have forgiven all my sins by dying and coming back to life again for me. I trust you and ask you to be the Lord of my life. I surrender my life to you. You are my God, my Savior, and my Lord. Let me experience your love and your good plans for my life! Amen. If you prayed that prayer, I believe that you got saved and you have secured your place in eternity (Heaven) with Jesus Christ.

If this is the first time you've prayed such a prayer, then I encourage you to reach out to a local church and let them know that you made this decision so that they can come alongside you and help you grow in your relationship with Jesus Christ, or you can text **GoFCA to 46322** to receive text messages with instructions to help you grow in your relationship with Jesus. Deciding to accept Jesus Christ as your Lord and Savior is the biggest decision that you will ever make in your life. Don't go another day without knowing that you know where you will spend eternity. We are not guaranteed another breath here on this earth. There's nothing more important in your life than to have a sense of urgency about accepting Jesus Christ as your Lord and Savior.

- We can't put it off for us or others.
- Eternity is real.
- Heaven is free. All you have to do is ask.
- What are your next steps?

Reflection

A sense of urgency is important in sports and your daily lives when it comes to certain situations. As you've seen in this section, the greatest sense of urgency in your life needs to be accepting Jesus Christ as your Lord and Savior and putting God first in all you do. If you have not accepted Jesus, write down everything you can think of that is keeping you from doing that now. Are the reasons that you haven't legitimate? Are there questions that you need to have answered? If so, reach out to someone that is a Christian friend, and get them to help you gain clarity.

If you have already accepted Jesus, then I encourage you to share your testimony and faith with as many people as you can for the rest of your life.

Mark 8:6 says, "What good is it for someone to gain the whole world, yet forfeit their soul?" 1 **Thessalonians 5:2** says," For you are fully aware that the Lord will come like a thief in the night! No one knows the day or hour." What do these two verses mean to you?

Sense of Urgency Notes:

Epilogue

Thank you for taking the Athletes Challenge! It is my prayer for you that you go back and look at the reflection section from every devotion and try to apply those principles to your life. I believe that these principles can make you a better student, athlete, family member, member of society, and Christian! As you read in the final section, the most important decision you can make in your life is to accept Jesus Christ as your personal savior and follow him for the rest of your life. Doing everything for the rest of your life for the glory of God will not come back void.

About the Author

BJ Laughter is the son of life-long educators, which helped mold his passion for young people. BJ earned degrees from Mars Hill and Gardner-Webb Universities and had an incredible career in public education as a teacher, coach, athletic director, and principal. Upon retirement in December 2019, he joined the Fellowship of Christian Athletes staff full-time as an area representative in southwest North Carolina. BJ resides in Hendersonville, North Carolina with his wife of almost thirty years, Amy, and he has one daughter, Emma, a senior at the University of Tennessee. BJ has a passion for helping young people to excel, not only in athletics but also in their school lives, family lives, community lives, and in their faith journey.